ESSENCE-PRESENCE-RADIANCE

ESSENCE-PRESENCE-RADIANCE

Being Beyond Our Own Limits

Shankari

Waterside Productions

Painting featured on cover art by Abhaya

First Printing, 2023

ISBN-13: 978-1-962984-08-9 print edition
ISBN-13: 978-1-962984-09-6 e-book edition

Waterside Productions
2055 Oxford Ave
Cardiff, CA 92007
www.waterside.com

DEDICATED TO ABHAYA,
MY BELOVED AND
JOURNEY PARTNER

ACKNOWLEDGMENTS

To all of you who have contributed in so many ways, supporting us and making this part of the journey easier to transit.

With deep gratitude to each of you.

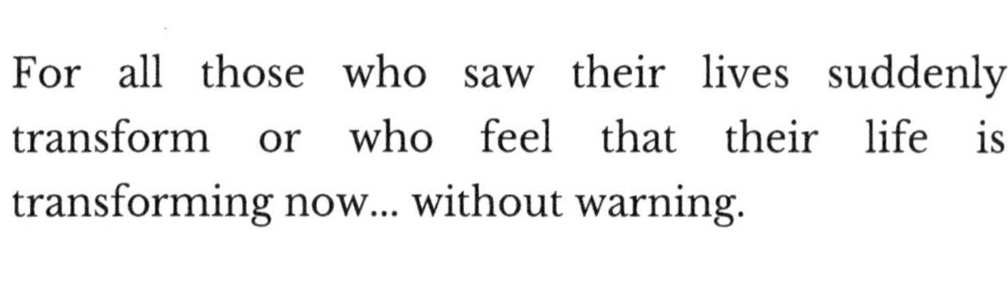

For all those who saw their lives suddenly transform or who feel that their life is transforming now... without warning.

TABLE OF CONTENTS

Part III: Radiance

ACCEPTANCE

And if everything is perfect as it is?

How difficult it is to accept reality when our soul just wants to fly and remember its true limitless and great nature. We are immense, even though everything around us tries to make us believe that we are small. We are not.

When our path is clear of obstacles, we embrace a different way of being in the world. We are happy, we believe in ourselves, and we are aware that we are making progress. The traffic light is green, and we are heading in the direction we want to go. A frequency that makes us expansive and creative, that makes us realize that we are part of a whole, and we contribute with our part, with our *presence*.

It is like removing the dust that caresses superficial ideas to shelter the truth that lives in our hearts. This does not appear pure because we have become accustomed to covering it with the clothing of fear. That disturbing companion that clouds our possibilities and potential and obscures the light of our own vital energy. Without fear, we move freely forward, and with fear, we simply do not advance or go back to unsuspected places.

Don't let the boat of existence navigate undesirable waters. Be the captain of your destiny and the leader of your own life. If you are not the protagonist of your own life, who is occupying that place? Why be the supporting actor in your own script? What or who are you giving that power to?

The problem is not in leading but in not knowing where we are headed. Choose your goal—that new aspect of yourself that you want to explore—and venture out to discover it. Whether the motor that moves you is something material or spiritual, only through practice can you achieve a degree of mastery in that experience.

It's like a professional athlete who needs to train over and over again to maintain that level of self-improvement. Practice gives us the key, and when we learn to do it correctly, our unlimited potential unfolds before us, and we realize that there is no limit.

Our way of thinking, feeling, or perceiving reality is the only obstacle that, once overcome, shows us a much broader field of always latent possibilities waiting to be chosen through where we focus or place our attention, our conscious or unconscious decisions, our personal code of interpretation, etc. They are all there vibrating at the same time until our thought or feeling chooses it as a reality that we later see reflected and materialized in our world. It is difficult for us to accept this, especially when we do not like what we have become or a reality that seems very different from what we had wanted.

As a gardener cares for and waters his seeds so that they germinate, so we water the seeds of love, gratitude, peace, joy, anger, hate, sadness, etc. Even two people under the same circumstances respond differently.

That is the difference: even though it is subtle, it is very far from where we wanted to be. Our commitment to how we perceive the world dictates the script we play. We have to rehearse, that is, carry out our practice of achieving those habits that are appropriate for what we are destined to be, to offer our value to the world, that unique and non-transferable value that each one of us carries.

We are all players in this game we call life; we only play a role. But we strive to make it the best role we can play. With that, we can walk our path with peace, happiness, and joy, inspiring others with our *essence,* with what connects us with what is authentic and divine in each of us. Our seed opens and spreads in the infinite terrain of consciousness, and we explore what was only a glimpse of light to become a crystal or prism through which light passes and separates into all colours and inexhaustible possibilities.

Then we are no longer subject to being puppets or repeating what others discover, but to finding out for ourselves. An authentic, direct experience of truth.

Lucia was astonished to see how she could understand that all of existence moved before her eyes in a way that in turn contained everything. It is as if she had access to a photograph showing all the separate pieces of the puzzle, waiting only for her to put them together to tell the story as she was been experienced it.

In the moments of greatest tragedy and challenge in our lives, we can obtain the nectar of understanding. There she was, and everything made sense when she was able to observe it with a broad perspective of the Self and not of the person.

But before this happened, she had to cross an inhospitable and unknown terrain until then to her when she saw how everything that was part of her reality at that moment vanished from her life, with hardly any warning.

It all started with a resounding fall that, like in Alice's tale in Wonderland, made Lucia go down the rabbit hole. In a flash of eternal time, all her little world fell, and she didn't know in what reality she found herself.

What does someone need to know who has left behind in a few seconds a whole life sharing an extraordinary love and is still alive without knowing exactly for what purpose? Even when that, it is not important. Who do you say that it's over, that the game is finished for you, that it stops the world, and that you simply want to get off? To surrender and accept what is happening without complaining or expecting anything; just being. Without even being able to protest, you just have to be part, but of what? If the roles are distributed, what is yours? Life gave you a new character, and you didn't even know it. But do you have to interpret it? Direct questions, without shortcuts continually haunted Lucia's mind.

She then remembered something important along the way: in moments of confusion, it is best to do nothing, just wait. The wheel will turn again, and maybe then I'll know what I need to do, she considered.

Once she stopped searching, wanting to change, transform, or control the experience that was taking place in her life, she began to hear a tiny voice, barely perceptible, but forceful, that reminded her of something more sacred, something that is broader than a specific moment in time... She remembered who she was, she remembered that beyond the roles we play in our lives and societies, there is an *essence*, something pure, that is not modified, that does not change over time, and she remembered why she loved so much. She remembered what made her life special and why, beyond the circumstances that love was still present in her heart. Nothing had changed it, not even death.

Beyond the noise, the lights, and the shadows that distract us, we shine the truth of who we are, and that truth is always there, but it becomes more evident and purer when we have fully surrendered to this game that we call life, together with its great and inseparable traveling companion that is death.

Lucia then realized that the more she knew about the nature and the true substance of which death is made, the more alive she was. She knew that it is not about how many years we accumulate in life, but about the ability to embrace it with everything she has for us. Discovering that living is knowing yourself, is touching the threads of existence without limits or filters. It is a direct experience that makes you shine, makes you love yourself more than you have ever loved yourself.

Lucia began to tear the veil of her superficial personality acquired over time through belief labels that she had not even contrasted but that had emerged as her own identity, because, up until that moment, they had served her. But when that identity faltered, she realized there was something else.

At the deep, unfathomable centre of her being, there was something untouched. Like an oasis in the middle of a desert where nothing made sense, there was something that gave value to her life. She did not know at that moment what it could be, nor could she even imagine, that it was only the beginning of something immeasurable. Something intimate, eternal, pure. Yes, Love..

How not? How was it going to get lost? Either it's in you or you can't love, it's that simple. We all have that flame, which is what makes us live and be present. That love does not belong to anyone or anything, that is what is special.

It is there for you, whatever your condition, nationality, gender, or profession. It is not true that we come with nothing and leave with nothing. We come with all the clothes of our own existence. In our garden there are all the seeds, and that of love is one of those that always sprouts because it is the substance on which life itself is sustained, from which it is nourished and grows. Living without love is not living. We don't necessarily have to love another person. Love does not distinguish; it only expresses itself. Either it is flowing through you or you are just asleep.

"It is not what happens in our lives that determines our destiny, but what we do with what has happened to us."

Perhaps we all die at some point in our journey and experience that transformation which may not be physical but of consciousness, and that changes everything; you just can't be the same anymore. There are many things that we leave behind in order to move forward lighter, but sometimes it goes even deeper and there is a real death within us that gives way to a rebirth. To a new way of breathing and living, an awakening to a truth kept inside that waits in silence until the time comes to be revealed.

Lucia knew it; she knew that she died that day, but she also knew that death did not take away Love, on the contrary, it made Love grow even more inside her. She was aware that when one loves something or someone, there is a separation between the one who loves and what is loved, but that separation in her case also vanished with events; only Love remained. Not to this or to that. Only Love. And in that moment, she understood that every step of the path she had walked, every decision and choice she had made, had prepared her for this moment.

Recognize the identity that goes beyond the person. The identity of something that has no form but is present in our *essence.* It is what we are, it is what we live for, and it is the fundamental engine of life. It is Love. Simply Love.

And as bearers of an Olympic torch, it does not distinguish between borders or forms, it moves in an invisible frequency, the substratum that gives us wings beyond our limited legs. The heart has spoken, and silence has accompanied it, whispering the secret melody beyond the echo of time. And there we remember that we are alive; butterflies hover around our plexus with a sensation of freshness, the *essence* that brings us back to the present moment and makes us *radiate* the light of awakening in ourselves. The brilliance that a new dawn brings, and even when Lucia could not see the horizon, she began to let herself marinate in that *essence* until she disappeared in it. Melting, timeless, and formless.

At that point in the journey where there is no path, it is best to stop, not to strategize forward, but to listen. When we let the noise of our mind and thoughts stop ringing and pass by, there is a moment, which can be extended in time, in which you only listen to your heart. It is "a feeling". You don't necessarily know what to do, but you recognize that it is an old friend you can trust. That you can listen to him and that he will give you some guidance or generous advice.

Because our heart is generous. The language of the mind is selfish, tries to control, and always profits. The language of the heart does not need to be the protagonist; it is just there for you, without asking or demanding anything, and is satisfied with very little. It is self-satisfied and always seeks to expand. The mind closes roads and the heart opens them. But like the two wings of a butterfly, we need both. Life is an adventure that sometimes takes us by surprise. But it's always waiting for us; it's not in a hurry.

When Lucia knew she could stop. Stop the "must" or "should"... and just relax into her own being, she began to wake up. Apparently, everything looked the same, but she had discovered what the warp and woof of existence is made of. And it was nothing like the truth she knew or the things she had previously given importance to.

So obvious and simple in its nature that she could hardly recognize it. And yet it is so vital, so real, that it goes unnoticed. It is not that it is hidden; on the contrary, it is so obvious, but the noise of our voices and the distractions to which we are subjected, spinning at a dizzying pace, make us not even notice.

In these times that we have had to witness, we have connected with everyone and everything, but we have disconnected from ourselves. We have forgotten to listen to our own voice. We don't have time for something so insignificant. Insignificant? Lucia wondered, If I think I'm insignificant or that my existence has no value, that sounds like I'm in trouble—she thought. If we do not love and know ourselves, how we are going to love and know others, or the world, the one we want to change without even having been introduced...

Lucia did not feel that she had lost anything because she did not feel separated from what she had loved, but she did recognize that her identity was being transformed. She then warned that in order to have a new identity, one must first know oneself. Because what is really being transformed? Again, silence took over the moment, and flooding everything, she soothed and calmed her agitated breathing.

Now there was something she didn't count on. Something had been revealed to her, and she needed to scrutinize all that it meant at this point in her journey.

If we have to carry a frequency, choose that this be the frequency of Love. And that is what Lucia chose, without hesitation, when she decided that it was the only thing of value that remained in her, the only truth, that contained the *essence*, the soul, on which the woof of life is made. At that moment, she realized that she was ready to share it...

PART I
ESSENCE

CONNECTING WITH OUR ESSENCE: LISTENING TO THE INNER VOICE

Connecting with our *essence* means listening within and at the same time being able to express our own voice, which in many cases goes beyond words and reveals the value and truth of who we are.

Expressing our true identity is as vital as breathing. Manifesting the truth that is within us allows us to connect with a sense of belonging, of integration. Like an orchestra, where each component represents and plays its music in unison and in complete communion with the rest. When that music is playing, at that moment, everything is harmonious, a single sound that comes from the union of all its members. There are no separate parts. It's a whole.

Our *essence* is this unique contribution to universal sound. It gives meaning to everything. Connecting with our *essence* is the beginning of the path of our inner search. For it is what gives meaning to our lives.

"*The journey of a thousand miles begins with one step.* - Lao Tse -

To know where we are going, we must first know ourselves. We must know where we are to discover the nature of our dreams and our potential. It is about connecting our inner compass and knowing our deepest truth - who we really are...

What is the source from which we come and what gives meaning to our whole life? What makes us happy, unique and special? What makes our soul sing? Our *essence* is the truth that lives within each of us and is perfect in itself. We just need to rediscover it. We allow our inner voice to express itself in the world.

We all play a unique role and diversity is essential. If we were all the same, or if we were all born to think and express ourselves in the same way, we would be like robots... How would that fit into human evolution, different cultures and traditions?

That is why it is so important to listen to our own inner voice and express the truth that makes us unique in the world. Because this is something that no one else can do for us; only we can do it.

How much have you been willing to be silent in order to have or keep something? How much have you silenced your own voice and personal expression?

It's easy to see, because when we don't listen to our own inner guidance, we become this pressure cooker in which we just explode, either through anger, frustration or other destructive ways of ourselves; or through depression, in which we just disappear and silence our inner sound, our own voice... We disappear and are silenced by the global sound of society and its own rhythm. But where does singularity fit in? Do we need to ask permission to be who we really are?

Diversity, like the great orchestra, contains all opinions, and all are valid because none is complete in itself.
As in the parable of the blind men and the elephant, absolute truth corresponds to a greater understanding than subjective truth.

This parable tells the story of a group of blind men who have never seen an elephant before, and who learn and imagine what the elephant is like by touching it. Each blind man feels a different part of the elephant's body, but only one part, such as the side or the tusk. They then describe the elephant based on their limited experience, and their descriptions of the elephant are different from each other.

The first person whose hand touched the trunk said, "This being is like a thick snake. To another person whose hand reached his ear, it looked like a kind of fan. Another person whose hand was on his leg said, "The elephant is a pillar like the trunk of a tree. The blind man who put his hand on his side said that the elephant was "a wall. Another who felt his tail described it as a rope. The last one who felt its tusk said that the elephant is that which is hard, smooth, and like a spear.

The Buddhist text Tittha Sutta, Udāna 6.4, Khuddaka Nikaya, dated around c. 500 BCE, during the Buddha's lifetime, contains one of the earliest versions of the story.

We humans have a tendency to claim absolute truth based on our limited subjective experience, while ignoring other people's subjective experiences that may be equally true. A world full of complementary opinions and different ways of doing and understanding things is a rich, abundant, expansive world... It does not accept judgment or comparison. It just is. A rose does not try to be another flower; it simply spreads its fragrance wherever it is in a vast universe that expresses and evolves.

Connecting to our *essence* connects us to our true nature: expansive, creative, free, and abundant. The door to the heart is our map and our inner guide. When we listen carefully to our own inner voice, we enter the paradise of our own existence.

Then we regain the ability to focus on what is of value to us. Our "little truth," which in turn is connected to the universal truth, makes that eternal and harmonious symphony sound in which we flow and participate in life. We feel alive and authentic. We have begun to listen for the signs, the answers and the guidance of what we want to know or experience. The path is clear and we know where we are going.

We reconnect with our inner voice, a sacred communication whose echo always remains alive in our hearts until we give it the space to be expressed. Great joy and success are generated in all that we do and express. We shine with the light of our own *essence*, who we really are, bringing richness and value to everything we do and the experiences of our lives.

BEYOND BEING LOST: EMBRACING CHANGE

The feeling of getting lost or being lost is a great opportunity to rediscover ourselves. We don't have to be afraid of it.

It is a mental concept because if you think about it, what or who are we losing? Is it because we don't know where we're going or because we feel like we're always in the same place?

Sometimes we feel as if we are in the same space or situation over and over again or that we are going around in the same circle, as if we are not moving forward. Everything seems to be repeating itself —the same experiences, the same conflicts, or similar relationships that we attract into our lives. It's just a big red signal that it's time to go one step further than usual. When the reality we are being shown is no longer serving us, something has to change.

It is not about letting go of everything and going somewhere else; it is more of a state of consciousness that tells us that we are ready to explore new goals or proposals, be it in some aspect of our life or in what we do. Because what is important is not what we do. It is how we do it, the quality we put into it, that makes the difference. And when our *presence* is no longer there, what we do has no value to us.

We do not have to wait until we have to make a radical change and leave everything all at once, although sometimes that is necessary, but we can begin to become aware that something needs to change within us and begin to take small steps, even minimal ones, that will bring us closer to a new state that is more in tune with ourselves again.

At other times, we realize that we are ready to take a bigger leap or venture into the unknown.

We are constantly evolving, so it is normal that we cannot always stay at the same level. With the

same beliefs, the same relationships, and the same repetitive thoughts.
The impermanent nature of life makes us constantly change. Nothing is always in the same state, nor are we the same as we were a few years ago. We grow, evolve and change. The important thing is that it is for something better. And that is where our power of choice lies.

A smooth and natural way to flow with life and the processes of change is to simply listen and embrace these moments as they come into our lives. Without trying to run away, escape or hide them.

When something stops serving or working for us, we can try to maintain or control it as if nothing were happening. But it is inevitable that at some point we will stop and examine the message behind the situation.

If we listen to ourselves and observe what is out of place in us, we can understand it and begin to make changes that will gradually, without the need for a complete transformation, lead us to a new, more stable, healthier and happier state in our lives.

This is an invitation to walk the path in a much smoother and easier way than if we don't want to hear that call or disconnect from that voice that warns us that something is no longer working.

Because in those cases it is no longer a warning and life is simply choosing for us, but perhaps the sense of loss is greater there. To see ourselves forced, in many cases, to adapt to a new reality that we may not have chosen.

Don't wait to be pushed, listen to your inner messages and align your goals, habits and beliefs more with the present moment.

When we are honest with ourselves, everything flows more harmoniously because we are truly ready to make these new changes. We are mature and ready to move into a more evolved state of ourselves.

It is exactly the moment when we are called to expand and not remain contracted. It's time to let new ideas, new beliefs, new inspirations come to us. We go to what attracts us and we allow ourselves to be nourished by new ideas which, like fresh air, create a new space within us until we feel "at home" again.

We don't have to force anything or make any effort, just allow ourselves to naturally embrace these possibilities.

Once again, the suit is no longer uncomfortable or tight, and it adapts to our size because we have simply grown. We then return to being comfortable in this new chapter of our life, work, relationships, or any other aspect that requires our attention.

If we wanted to stay in the same state of consciousness without evolving, it's like telling life that we already know everything. We are so full that there is no room for anything new. But we complain that nothing original goes on, and what happens is that we repeat the same cycles over and over again.

When we learn, we are renewing ourselves, embracing the ever-changing life, and adapting to the new opportunities and experiences that naturally open up and that would otherwise be impossible to bring into our lives.

You've probably had an episode where something important changed in you, and even if it was intense or painful, you know that in the end it brought truly extraordinary things into your life. Allow yourself to be surprised again. Every day is a new opportunity to change, to move forward, to embrace a new experience or a new way of understanding life... There are no limits. Limitations exist only in your mind.

There is a saying that "some are born with a star and others starred" but really we are all under the same star, under the same sun. And what we do with the time we are given depends on us, on our attitude to life, not on what we are ordered to do. We can always go beyond our own limits, beyond ourselves and our beliefs.

And maybe life will surprise you. In any case, if you're not in a good place right now, you don't have much to lose. If not now, when?

Take those small steps and introduce new actions and practices that inspire or motivate you and allow you to move toward a new reality that is more in line with what makes you happy and what makes you alive and present.

The feeling of loss or being lost disappears because it isn't real; it was just an invitation to move forward, to surpass yourself.

THE INITIATION PROCESS: ANSWERING THE CALL

The initiation process involves starting from scratch. Something has happened, or many things have happened at once, and everything has stopped working for you. You are back at square one. You can't keep playing the same game as before; you can't keep doing the same things the way you did them. They are those moments where something has definitely changed within you and completely shaken your foundations, your beliefs, and your values. Those moments when you need to re-evaluate everything.

It may be that this initiation process, or inner calling, was caused by a great material or personal loss or by a combination of events, but the important thing is not what caused it but what it means to you.

Normally, it is a deep process of consciousness, or spiritual transformation, that takes you to another level. And it doesn't just affect one aspect of your life; it touches them all at once. On a personal level, in relationships, at work, and in what you do in life.

That's why it doesn't matter what brought you here, it's just a deep feeling of being upside down and nothing working the way it used to.

It has more to do with your identity and how you perceive the world. Because what, until now, had value for you simply no longer has it. The feeling of loss is complete, but it goes beyond being lost.

Something in you needs to evolve; you recognize that call inside you, that you know you can't postpone, and that you must heed it. A call to do something different, even if you don't know what. Then you feel that something inside you has to change and you have to start again. It is a process with yourself; it has nothing to do with others or external circumstances, but you have to discover what it is that has stopped working within you.

It's about those moments when you have a strange feeling that can express itself in you in different ways. Do you recognize those moments when it seems like all the cars are coming straight ahead and the only one going in the opposite direction is you, or that you don't belong in this world, like you come from another planet, or that you must have been adopted because you don't fit into the family either, or just that everything you have built in your friendships, work relationships, and what you do simply doesn't work anymore.

A process of great transformation in the way you perceive your reality. But at the same time, it is a deep invitation within you that something needs to change.

It is as if the level of your consciousness in which you find yourself has reached an end, a dead end, in which there is no return, and you need to advance to a new level, expand your points of view, review what your priorities are, because these also evolve, and what the main values and priorities in your life are based on.

These are moments when life tests you because you are ready to go one step further than where you are currently. You are ready to pass the course; you cannot keep repeating the same subjects that you have already learned. You are simply ready to have new experiences in your life.

It is not necessarily about changing anything on the outside, leaving your friendship or family relationships, or simply venturing into the unknown. It is before this moment. It is a moment of reflection and an invitation to go inside. To observe and discover within yourself what it is that has become dislocated within you, that it no longer serves you, that no longer works. To be able to project new goals and introduce the changes that will lead you to achieve them.

It is time to let go of what you know and leave your comfort zone, not to anywhere, but to yourself. In deep listening that reveals and shows you a new understanding that is more in line with who you are in this moment.

Are you tired? Do you feel that you can't keep doing what you're doing and that you don't know where you are or what your role is?

Something inside of you is telling you that you cannot put it off, that you must embrace the inner transformation that has taken place in you and take the reins again, beyond the conditions and limitations, beyond the excuses. The time has come to gain a new insight and understanding that will allow you to be at peace with yourself and what surrounds you.

The initiation process is a very uncomfortable but brilliant and profound state in which we disidentify from who we thought we were or from the things that were important to us, as if we had to carry them in our backpack for life, and we simply allow ourselves to move forward without fear to a new level of understanding.

All the answers will be available to us; once we understand them, we will know what to do and how to resolve the situation. And it doesn't take any effort or anything external to change the circumstances. It is up to us to change ourselves. We will not stop being ourselves; on the contrary, we will become more authentic; we are simply changing our skin.

An invitation to embrace a new level of awareness, insight and understanding of ourselves and our surroundings.
We can insist on being the same person we always thought we were, but we simply aren't, and that's why we suffer. Our expectations are not being met because we insist on being or having something that simply isn't there. But the good news is that everything is easier than it seems. Even if we are sitting in complete darkness without seeing or understanding anything, it is only a matter of turning on the light that represents that awareness or understanding, and we will be able to see everything clearly from a different place. Then we will know what to do, where to go, and what our next step is.

In this initiation process, the only thing that is important is to allow ourselves to ask the appropriate questions instead of being carried away by emotions that disempower us, such as Why is this happening to me? Why can't I move forward? Why do I feel so different from everyone and everything else? Why don't I fit in? These questions only keep you in the challenge, but do not provide you with the solution. It seems that you keep hitting the same wall.

In this case, it would be better to ask questions that will help you increase your level of compression. For example, "What can I learn from this situation? How can I move forward? How do I get back to a place where everything flows and I feel happy and at peace? What values or beliefs do I need to change in order to access a new state of happiness and fulfillment in my life? What do I need to understand from this moment on? What is the invitation here?

When you realize this, you will have moved on from those kinds of questions that keep you in a position of victimization, of not having control, or of feeling like a cork in the middle of the sea being pounded by the waves, to regaining your power as a generator and creator of these changes.

Everything will have brought you back to a starting position, a starting square, where you have the game in front of you again, but you are setting new rules and ways of playing. You have the dice. And the game begins again; only now your knowledge and experience will allow you to play with an advantage.

That is when the initiation process ends, because you will have understood and embraced this new level of consciousness within you.

OPEN YOUR HANDS AND LET GO

If we want to be free, we have to let go; we have to open our hands. And to do that, there can be nothing contained in them, nothing attached, nothing to possess. This doesn't mean that we can't have the material things we want; it means that our consciousness can't be attached to them or to anything.

When we are aware that nothing belongs to us, we can open ourselves to abundance, and at the same time we are free. Otherwise, those same possessions end up possessing us; they enslave us to have and maintain them, or the fear of losing them paralyzes us, and we continue to postpone happiness in pursuit of I don't know what.

Open your hands, be free, and enjoy everything you have or possess, knowing that it will also be transformed, knowing that it is not yours, because even so it is gaining more value in you at this precise moment...

There is nothing to defend or fight for, not even our beliefs or opinions, which also evolve and change. Just being aware of embracing in every moment what we are and have right now... That gives us freedom; that allows us to move lightly, without ties, without fear.

Open your hands and trust, even when it seems impossible. Trust in what you can't see yet. That is faith; that is moving lightly in life, knowing that life is taking care of you at every moment.

There is a term from Africa called *'Ubuntu'* that has many meanings and connotations, but one of them is the feeling that no matter where you are or how alone you may seem, if the situation calls for it, wherever you are or in any corner of the world, there will always be someone or something to help you, and in the same way, you will always be able to help those who need it. When we join forces, we all win. We join the intelligence that is superior and that gives meaning to everything, beyond ourselves.

We are only passing through; what prevails is what we participate in. It is expressed only in you, without being possessed, without limits, without authorship, but thanks to your own existence and that of others, it can expand.

"Challenges become small in the face of love."

Love and its different facets, such as compassion, solidarity, esteem, trust, faith, etc., always begin with oneself and manifest themselves like a light in the face of darkness; it dissolves it, leaving only light. True love dissolves all fear without leaving a trace and disappears in its truth.

Open your hands knowing that the entire Universe is walking by your side; feel free; feel safe; move forward easily; don't hold on; don't cling to anything. Enjoy everything you have and everything you are in every moment and every moment will bring you what you need.

This is the *'Alchemy of Life'*, constantly transforming and refining, if we are aware and allow it, our own 'inner gold'.

TRANSCEND FEAR: TRUSTING IN THE UNKNOWN

Fear is a powerful emotion that works very similar to fire, consuming our energy as if it were the fuel that allows it, in just a few moments, to cease to be controllable, reducing all our power and potential to ashes.

Therefore, when we notice its presence, we do not try to hide or disguise it, but rather know that it is there before it begins to grow. We recognize that it is an emotion that has come to visit us, but we do not invite it to take up residence in our lives, for if we fuel it or let it grow within us, it will simply destroy everything in its path.

We can always maintain our power if we manage to do so, knowing that the situation we are facing with fear at that moment is simply conditioned by the emotion.

But we are not that emotion; it is just a state, and it is temporary if we make sure that it does not sit at our table. And we leave it out, like we leave our shoes out so as not to dirty our sanctuary, our home. We do not allow it to run our lives.

Fear only warns us and that is the true purpose of its nature. Instinctively or in survival mode, when we are faced with real danger, it usually lasts only a few moments and then we return to our natural state. When this does not happen, and we do not recover from this state, it is because the fear and stress generated by the situation has taken over.

Trying to solve a problem out of fear will inevitably lead us to failure. There are many ways to approach challenging situations with calm and self-control.

But it is something that needs to be practiced repeatedly so that when the moment of challenge comes, we can respond and not react.

It is then that the solution appears, precisely because of our attitude toward it. If we have not practiced being calm and collected, which can be through meditation, conscious breathing practices, or other different techniques that help us so that when the moment comes, we do not feel overwhelmed. Don't wait for moments when everything is ruined to act coherently and peacefully.

Conversely, when we are calm and peaceful, we can handle any situation that comes our way from a position of leadership. We lead our emotions, our thoughts and our attitudes, and that is the big difference. But we are no longer being dragged like pawns from one challenge to another in our lives. We go from choosing the move to spontaneously allowing the solution to show up without suffering or wasting our energy and time.

Each time we practice, as a healthy habit, we are investing in success to be able to face any challenge or situation that requires great attention on our part.

When we affirm or think, "I am afraid," it is like believing that the emotion is part of us when it is not. The more peace we generate and house within ourselves, the more energy comes back to us and we have more time and freedom.

Fear does not live in the present. It is only when we anticipate, when we worry about the future, that this emotion visits us or, in a short period of time, takes over our entire reality.

We have all experienced, to a greater or lesser extent, the havoc that fear can wreak in our lives. And when the situation is over, we are able to see that what we gave so much importance and power to did not have it, or we could have resolved it in a much simpler way.

We have gone from a state where fear was a basic and instinctive tool of man to survive, or in a situation of extreme danger, to another level where we constantly live in that state of survival, fleeing or reacting to everything, surviving. just with fear, as if it were natural, when it is not. We tend to run away from it by not wanting to face it, because often we don't even know how, or we choose to numb it with distractions, looking for a state of superficial happiness that allows us to get out of this cycle.

We have simply fallen prey to fear. It can be at a small level or continuously generate anxiety and chronic episodes of panic at a much more complex and deeper level.

But it is never too late to make the decision to change those habits and thoughts that have invited fear into our lives, not to prevent it, but to take over our healthy decision-making power and our ability to create and generate successful solutions.

The solution to any problem or difficult situation that needs to be addressed is always much easier than suggestions or actions that come from a state of fear, which often only make the situation worse.

Take a breath and go into your inner space, free of noise and distractions, until the emotion has passed. It's like taking refuge within yourself. If you notice, bamboo trees have the ability to be flexible, and when the wind blows, they bend until it passes, then they return to their natural position without breaking. This is what you can achieve if you dedicate or invest a little effort each day to help you be calm and at peace with yourself.

Phrases such as "I breathe in and I am aware of the fear; I breathe out and I relax the fear within me" Exercises inspired by the teachings of Master *Thich Nhat Hạnh* and other conscious breathing meditations can help us return to the present moment. Bring this *timing* to our attention.
The first thing you can do when you find yourself in a disturbing situation is to observe how you are reacting and whether you have opened the door to fear, or worse yet, invited it to stay. Remember that when you are present, in the moment of the here and now, all your *presence*, all your attention, all your awareness is with you, and in that moment there is no real fear of danger. It is an emotion, and if it is in you at that moment, it is because you have once again anticipated it with your mind and your thoughts, probably imagining the worst scenario that you are capable of imagining.

The good news is that it usually works that way with the same intensity, but conversely, when we realize that fear has visited us, we acknowledge it and focus on our breath, generating and creating a space of peace. Until we regain our ability to make the right decisions, we should observe and reflect on whether we need to do something with it or just let it go.

If you are watering a plant at this moment, you are not thinking about whether it is too much or too little water; you are just watering the plant. When you are finished, you can observe and determine if it needs more water or if it has enough. It is the same with our challenges: we observe them, we attend to them, and we do what is necessary to do, but we do not anticipate them or give them our power.

If you have practiced enough with the right tools or techniques to help you, it is not at all difficult to find the right solution. Like driving a car, you know that when you first learned to drive your gestures were abrupt and clumsy, but with practice they have become better. something mechanical and automatic that no longer requires all of your attention or energy to do properly.

As with great investments, the gift we receive from overcoming our own fears is that we accumulate confidence in ourselves and our own abilities, feeling increasingly prepared and brave in any situation we have to face. We do not hide, we do not flee, but we embrace fear, knowing that it is an emotion and that it is part of our path.

As we walk or move beyond our own fears and limitations, we discover that our perceptions of fear are only mental, and then we can observe where the source of our strength, courage and determination in life lies. It is our attitude toward it that changes everything.

Be encouraged to breathe beyond fear and discover that bravery and courage are never separate from you; they are always with you. It's just a matter of where you focus.

THE LIBERATING POWER OF FORGIVENESS

Forgiveness looks like a disguise, like a mask that, once put on, hides the true face of the wearer. For it seems that its frequency forces us to a place where our hearts do not want to go, but like that disguise, it contains the hidden gift of liberation.

It is difficult for us to forgive because it seems to our mind that we are justifying something that is not right, or because we do not want to be hurt again. When we reach a certain level of expansion and freedom from feeling hurt, we are not willing to give it up. However, it is exactly the opposite: staying in that level of awareness without moving forward, stuck in the past and in what has happened, that keeps us wounded.

When we can see our life as a path of evolution and learning, we begin to feel at peace with everything that has happened to us and that we have experienced. We know that in each moment we have done the best that our conscience allowed us to do, and this frees us.

"Forgiveness is an act of the heart,
not the mind."

We leave behind the weight of the past and embrace who we are in this moment. This allows us to let go and feel that there is no mistake and that we always have the opportunity to embrace each other and treat each other with love and respect beyond the events that have occurred.

Realizing this helps us to forgive ourselves; it is an act of pure love. Love without conditions, because we do not love each other for being perfect. When we love and respect each other with all our imperfections, we are admitting that we are humans. We are only here to learn, and forgiveness is precisely the key that allows us to love and accept ourselves as we are, including our most vulnerable parts. It's like letting go of a heavy backpack and moving lightly forward, knowing that every step of the way we grow, we evolve.

The act of forgiving ourselves makes it easier for us to forgive others because we also understand their mistakes and that anything that happened in the past is precisely from the past; it is no longer in our present. Just as we evolve, change, and improve, others also change and transform, and they are not the same as that image or slide that we freeze in our mind. By forgiving, we release those memories and stop attracting those experiences into our lives.

Let it go so that we no longer hold it with our thoughts or emotions. We stop giving it power in our lives.

There are people who say that "they forgive, but they do not forget." In that case, it is only half-forgiveness; if you see, there is something that continues to be withheld.

If you throw something you no longer want out of anger, resentment, etc., like a ball, it will bounce back to you. But if instead you let go with understanding and the determination to turn the page, it is like putting what you no longer want in your life, into the flow of a river, and with the intention of loving and respecting yourself above what happened, you recognize that you have learned from this experience... This act of love frees you. And like the river, it will continue its course, but it will not return to you or your present.

The wounds that still live in our hearts must always be healed by our understanding.
When we understand it with a broad vision that encompasses a love without limits that even allows us to put ourselves in the place of others in order to understand it, it is the greatest gift we can give ourselves.

Forgiveness is one of the greatest acts of unconditional love. It doesn't need an explanation, but it heals you. Heal your heart, and old wounds can heal, disappear, or remain only as witnesses to what we have been able to overcome.

"The wound is the place where the light enters." - Rumi -

One of the most significant effects we discover when we forgive is that obstacles disappear. The path is clear because we have stopped perpetuating those moments or experiences of imbalance in our lives.

We measure ourselves, and by forgiving ourselves and others, we are ready to move forward from a new level. We have learned and no longer need this type of experience in our lives. We close the chapter and live in the present, blessing each moment and knowing that we are free. A blank page no longer conditioned by what happened in the past. We love each other without the need to be perfect, just as we are.

Open your heart, look at your old wounds and don't let them hurt you anymore. Allow them to heal with love and compassion for yourself and others.

How much weight are you willing to release?

To forgive yourself and others, you don't have to know how to do it; you just have to set your intention, be willing, and allow it; then the path clears itself.

You can even forgive others without seeing them or telling them in person, just by doing it in your heart. Opening yourself to allow whatever happened to be healed by love and the act or willingness to make it so.
When we forgive, we recognize that we are more than what has happened or the circumstances that have occurred in our lives.

We recognize that we are more than our old wounds and that love is the power that lives within us that heals everything, including what has hurt us.

When we do this, we allow that love to penetrate us and set us free.

There is always an opportunity for a new moment for anyone who is courageous and forgives themselves with understanding and compassion.

Don't believe these words! Try it for yourself! Let go and forgive the old wounds in your heart and allow the footprints on the path that you leave with your new steps to reflect lightness, love and peace. They are the sign of a new feeling...

Don't bring anything from the past with you; just recognize this moment in time as something sacred, which is what it really is.

If you are not able to accept whatever happened in your past, it is as if your life stops there. You will be trapped in that situation, reliving it over and over again. Moving on is easier than it seems. Even if you don't know how, get out of the loop that keeps your consciousness trapped in circumstances from the past. Simply activating your intention to leave it behind is enough.

You begin to take one step out, then another, and when you realize that your energy is no longer involved, it is more current, fresh, and light. A strange thing happens: you learn from past experiences, and your level of maturity clears your path to a place of greater harmony and renewed balance.
Take the initiative to forgive yourself for past mistakes and the mistakes of others!

Take back the reins and stop playing the same old movie over and over again in your consciousness. Rewrite your script from where you are in this moment, with what you have learned along the way, but light and fresh for what you are experiencing now.

Be the best version of yourself; only you can choose that. When you forgive, all the held energy is released and available, like a great source and reserve of love, just waiting for you to choose to release it.

THE LANGUAGE OF RELATIONSHIPS

If there is anyone - a teacher - who teaches us about ourselves, that teacher is our relationship.

We tend to think of relationships as being with others or with the outside world, but the most enduring relationship that accompanies us throughout our lives, the most authentic relationship, is the relationship we have with ourselves. It is important that this relationship with ourselves is open, honest and sincere. Because it is the pillar on which the other relationships we establish with the environment and with others are based.

If we don't know ourselves, if we don't respect ourselves, or if we don't have trust and love for ourselves, how can we have it for others?

We have to make sure that we have fluid communication and the necessary space to create the habit of listening to our inner messages. The relationship with our body, which is always communicating with us; the relationship with our emotions and thoughts, which guide the direction of our life; our deepest desires, etc. And giving ourselves the support to understand or remember that we are constantly changing and what was valid some time ago may no longer be valid. We are free to change, evolve and transform.

There are several valuable techniques for listening to your voice and communicating with yourself:

One that 'makes a difference' is creating a healthy intimate space. Your '*little oasis*' at home... A small corner or room of the house that becomes your little corner, your personal sanctuary... You create an intimate space where you feel safe, a place that you can prepare with the things that make you feel calm and at peace (with a comfortable chair, large plants, candles, aromas, etc.) and that you can return to every day to rest and reconnect with yourself, even if it is only for a few minutes, because what makes it useful is its regularity. When you enter this sanctuary, you know that it is a time for you to listen to inspiring music, follow a guided meditation with a specific purpose, or engage in any other practice that raises your frequency and helps you relax.

Another very important technique is writing, either as a journal reflecting your impressions, or by asking yourself questions that you answer from a calm and reflective place. In this case, we are using writing as a regular tool to communicate our needs - something that seems very simple, but at the same time is tremendously powerful and therapeutic, because it helps you to express yourself, to get to know yourself better, and to establish a friendly and respectful relationship with yourself.

We cannot wait for moments when we are in trouble to establish internal communication. It is more powerful, as in any relationship, if we cultivate it frequently, because in the moments when everything is shaking inside us, we will know what to do. We will have the habit of going to our sanctuary or our inner oasis and taking a breath. This is where new ideas come from, or we can understand what needs to be addressed within ourselves before blaming or holding others responsible for what is unbalanced within us.

When we notice that we are at odds with others or that everything is becoming a challenge and even our electronic devices are responsible for waging "war" on us, it is time to stop and observe what frequency we are tuning to through our thoughts and emotions.

In those moments when everything seems to be going against you, the only one going against the current is you. Even if you went to the most inhospitable and lonely corner of the planet, you would find some reason to feel bad because your emotional and mental state goes with you wherever you go.

An example that illustrates this is the parable of the empty ship by *Thich Nhat Hanh*:

A monk decides to meditate alone, away from his monastery. He takes his boat out to the middle of the lake, moors it there, closes his eyes and begins his meditation.
After a few hours of undisturbed silence, he suddenly feels the bump of another boat colliding with his own.

With his eyes still closed, he senses his anger rising, and by the time he opens his eyes, he is ready to scream at the boatman who dared disturb his meditation.
But when he opens his eyes, he sees it is an empty boat that had probably got untethered and floated to the middle of the lake.
At that moment, the monk achieves self-realization, and understands that the anger is within him; it merely needs the bump of an external object to provoke it out of him.
From then on, whenever he came across someone who irritated him or provoked him to anger, he reminded himself:
"The other person is merely an empty boat. The anger is within me..."

People who know themselves and are solid in their relationships with themselves tend to have successful and healthy relationships with others based on self-esteem and self-confidence.

Sometimes it's just a readjustment or reevaluation to get back in tune with our own frequency. Like a radio station, we return to our center and reconnect with that source and oasis of inner peace that we cannot maintain permanently or store in a little jar for when we need it, but which

is always available and can be accessed at any time with our attention.
We flow and dance in constant movement with life instead of pretending that the whole universe adapts to us and trying to control reality or others to achieve it. In movement and fluidity there is freedom, expansion and flexibility. In rigidity there is stagnation and contraction, and we lose our power and energy.

The relationship we establish with ourselves is one of unlimited potential that will never let us down. It is like embracing our most vulnerable part and being there, present, for everything that happens, without going to war with any aspect, but rather accepting and understanding its nature with compassion. Like the friend we hug when he or she is in trouble, simply by remembering that they are not alone. The more love and compassion we have for ourselves, the greater our capacity to love and be generous with everything around us.

PART II
PRESENCE

THE GRACE OF THE PRESENT MOMENT

If we are not present with our full attention in this moment, we miss the *essence* of life and the grace contained in each moment.

We cannot segment our lives and leave these moments for when we are on vacation, when we allow ourselves to relax and breathe more deeply.

It doesn't matter what responsibilities or events fill our days and schedules; we can always place ourselves in the present moment we are experiencing in order to live it fully through our awareness.

This ability to bring ourselves to focus on the present moment needs to be practiced. A few minutes each day to allow ourselves this space of conscious and awake attention can transform our entire day, making it lighter, fresher, and more productive. When we are more present, we have more energy and are more decisive.

Even if you are in the middle of an important meeting or a challenging situation, you can always take a few seconds to go to the bathroom or take some space, breathe deeply, invite your attention back to the present moment, to your body, to your emotions, and observe what is happening inside of you. When you return to the meeting or situation you were in, you will find that you are in a different situation. Calmer and more practical, with more breadth and perspective, because your power to act is only in the present moment.

A power and frequency that you regain through your breath and consciousness when you tune in and synchronize with this moment that is unique, unrepeatable and sacred.

If you have arranged to meet a friend, and you take the train, but you get off one stop early (anticipating the future) or one stop late (as if revisiting the past), you simply don't make it to your appointment. Your friend, like your power or ability to be decisive, was waiting for you at the appointed place, that is, in the present moment, but you could not find him because you were not attentive.

The more anxious and stressed (future) or depressed (past) we are, the less we enjoy the *essence* that only reveals itself in the present moment. The only moment over which we have power through our consciousness.

Follow me for a moment with this ***practice***:

Close your eyes and take a deep breath. Acknowledge and become aware of this moment. Put all your attention on what you perceive within yourself; how is your breath?
Notice if it is short, if it is long, if you feel restless, if there is any physical discomfort. What attracts your attention?

Now exhale deeply but very slowly, as slowly as you can, letting the air out little by little, like a balloon that you are letting go of until you feel that your lungs are completely empty.

This is an opportunity to let go of the old air in your lungs and regenerate yourself with a new and fresh space where the new oxygen from your next deep breath will fill your lungs again. Repeat in a sequence of 5 or 6 times in a roll, and when you are finished, see how you feel.

This practice takes only a few seconds, and the most amazing thing is that it is something we do from the moment we enter the world with our first breath until our last breath. Breathing is a continuous act throughout our lives; the difference here is that we do it consciously. With our attention we use the air to fill ourselves with the new and let go of the stress, anxiety, depression or sadness that connects us to the old.

There is no effort when we use conscious breathing as a tool to help us be in the right station of the present moment. We simply use our attention and awareness to do so and then regain our mastery and ability to resolve the most complicated or stressful situations in our lives, which are precisely the ones that require the most energy from us. And that is when we need the most serenity to handle the moment appropriately.

Have you ever been in the *presence* of a person who manages everything with great skill and extraordinary peace, even in very difficult situations or situations that require a lot of responsibility, and continues to be a true leader, knowing what to do at all times? When we look at them from the outside, it seems extraordinary to us how they can have such peace or serenity. But the only difference with another person who does not have it is the practice of being present with their conscious attention and getting off at the right stop.

It is when you can perceive the "grace" of the moment, beyond what is happening around us.

A new inspiration, a new moment, a new opportunity to fill ourselves with the new, the fresh...

A new exhalation, a letting go of what we no longer need, and an opening to the available peace that the present moment brings us.

SAILING INTO THE UNKNOWN: BE BRAVE

The fear of leaving our comfort zone is like a bird jumping into the void and opening its wings to fly.

We really remain just as safe, because the insecurity that holds us back belongs only to the mind, to the realm of thoughts and beliefs that we have about ourselves and about the world. But we are not that; we are more.

Just a few seconds of courage - to hold our breath and dare to move forward - to swim a little deeper into the unknown.

We leave behind the apparent security that seems to continue to rule our lives, when inside we know that we are only circling the same familiar waters over and over again, that we are trapped in a routine that does not advance, that it hurts to breathe.

And what if it is only a limitation caused by our way of thinking? What if we allow ourselves to go further, to embrace each day with a new and fresh emotion, remembering that life is a great adventure, that it has no form, only what we want to give it?

Like playing with clay, thoughts create our reality. But if we allow ourselves to be guided beyond what is known and what is already created, the new form of what we are capable of conceiving can also transcend all our little known seas and reconnect with the source, that limitless ocean.

Then we can't stop creating - one idea, then another, a dream come true, and then another that surpasses the previous one. We create, we create, and we create without stopping, because we have rejoined the river of creation, the world that flows without stopping, whether we use it or not.
The adventure of life is not confined to spending the years in a script that we have not even written, in which we only continue to sleep in that drowsiness in which we simply survive.

Something is pushing us to go on, and something is holding us back, preventing us from moving forward into the unknown.

It is time to breathe and to tune the beat of our vital rhythm to the rhythm of life and the universe. And we surely know that we are ready to move confidently and naturally into deeper waters.

It is more worth living a short time, drinking the nectar of life, feeling completely alive, and loving bravely without limits, even for a few minutes, rather than not knowing what love is. Yes, you have to be brave, and sometimes it hurts, but the real thing is the direct experience with life, requires us to know ourselves, love ourselves, and embrace ourselves with all our imperfections.

"You can't swim and have your clothes dry", but you can swim naked, with nothing to hide, with all your honesty. Express your truth, because then life will also show you its truth, and like two lovers who meet, you will feel what it is to be alive and what love is beyond this or that, pure love, beauty, and bliss.

It is the *essence* of our own authenticity, which shines and shows itself with all its imperfections, knowing that we are not what we thought we were and that we have no limits.

We fly free, with a complete opening of the heart, and everything we are capable of creating, when we get rid of our own insecurities, make-up, labels, and protections that do not allow us to move lighter. When we are able to open our hearts and love with all our truth without expecting anything in return, just for the pleasure of loving and being loved, we float with open arms in the ocean of creation. Every day is a new adventure, and the freshness of the moment is renewed.

You will enter a space of pure creation. You will feel life renewing itself within you and guiding you towards something original that is yet to be explored. Something unique, but that will be revealed to you. It is the space where everything is created. You are entering the Kingdom of God, in the image and likeness of him. Then everything that had not yet materialized or possible, in the human mind, becomes tangible, and we say:

Ah, a miracle!

Yes, the miracle of life, of being alive, is for those who have the courage to transcend their own limits, not only for themselves but for others. true service. A footprint that inspires others to navigate the ocean of existence with determination, courage, and perseverance.

Allow the sacred to settle in our hearts and take the reins.

Like a powerful captain who always knows what he has to do, even though he would never have sailed in those waters before.

It is the wisdom itself that has survived intellectual knowledge, and from the bowels, from the depth of being, it creates a new solution, a new way to walk the path.

You will have become a teacher, and your own direct experience of life will have taught you to trust, to be attentive to signs, and to open yourself to the limitless, to what has no form, no name, and no time.

All inventions, creations, technological advances, art, and even ideas that generate abundance come from this place, from the inexhaustible, free, and ownerless source... The Universe has no 'copyright'. Because it is alive, dynamic, and changing, and because it is limitless, immeasurable in its own creation, pure consciousness.

Later, others will want to copy, possess, etc. But happiness lies in one's own originality and unique creations that do not belong to anyone or anything.
And like the sand mandalas designed by Tibetan monks, once created, you can delete it, because nothing ties you to something that is not yours. Everything is impermanent, and only in the act of the idea of being original, expansive, and of service is where the *essence* of what is created lies.

It's pure, innocent, spontaneous, original, and fresh, which is what makes it worth it. Pure life without beginning, without end. That moment when everything makes sense... Our efforts, our failures, and our falls to try again. That moment reminds us why it was so valid to walk the path, the value of the authentic... Pure love. True love.

The laughter that unexpectedly crosses your path and makes you smile—that moment in which you have surprised another with a special gift that was not expected, those moments of simplicity that fill our lives with a unique value, and we fall completely surrendered to love... We fall in love with life and with that sacred moment that is regenerated when we do not look for it or try to force anything; we just allow it to find us.

May it embrace us and remind us of the reason why we are here and for what. The true purpose of our lives.

Follow your passion; swim towards what keeps you alive and passionate about it. The truth of your heart without boundaries. Dare to dream, to discover for yourself that the only limits are in your mind.

Time is art; it reminds us of the Mayan civilization. What you do with it is what gives value to your life.

We do not have to repeat or settle, but remember that we are precious and eternal, and that everything has a purpose that makes us unique and special and that connects us with the divine and sacred; what cannot be possessed can only be experienced. That is our true, free, and expansive nature.

THE MIRROR OF REALITY: A FAITHFUL REFLECTION OF WHERE OUR CONSCIOUSNESS LIVES

Our life is like a faithful mirror that reflects exactly what we emit with our thoughts and beliefs, with our emotions and actions—a reflection of our consciousness and inner perception.

Often we do not like what we see, and we prefer to blame others or fight with the world instead of taking responsibility for our own actions and thoughts. This takes away our power, and from there it is very difficult to change the situation.

But if we look deeper, if we leave fear, judgment and guilt outside for a moment, and if we are brave enough to want to understand why our life is exactly the way it is, in that moment we will discover how we ourselves have contributed to creating this reality, which may not really be the one we wanted. The more honest we are, the more truthful the answer will be.

If we are fighting with ourselves internally and, instead of recognizing it, we throw all our anger outward, that is what life reflects in our scenario. As in the game of squash, the harder you throw the ball, the stronger its bounce will be...

But if, when we feel overwhelmed, we observe how our emotions, beliefs, and thoughts have taken the reins, directing us down the wrong path, we can stop for a moment and embrace those emotions as if they were that most vulnerable part of ourselves that simply needs our attention. It's like that little child who won't stop crying until he has your attention and you listen to him again.

There is no need to fight them, escape them, or run away from them. We all have the ability to manage our own emotions, no matter how difficult it may seem at times. And when we are able to recognize that they are there, when we are able to see what is wrong in ourselves or in our relationships, the situation changes, the child stops crying, and everything calms down. And what we need to change or improve happens naturally.

Sometimes it comes in the form of extra help and we find the right person or professional to guide us and help us focus and know what to do; other times it comes in the form of a message that comes directly to us through a book or a conversation and offers us the opportunity to become aware and find out what the appropriate steps would be to transform all those negative emotions into much healthier ones that bring into our lives the experience that we really want to live.

If we observe and face our reality with awareness, with attention and with the care it needs, that is what will be reflected in our lives.
As you water your seeds of love, understanding and kindness to yourself, these will be the fruits that you will see growing in your garden and in your experiences in life.

Doubt Is Under Observation

If you face your daily life with doubt, or if you doubt other people and their intentions, it will actually be reflected in your mirror and become reality. You have simply invited it with your conscience. But if you decide, even if you don't know how, to trust and decide to try again from a different perspective and a broader understanding, with more love and compassion and without any doubt, just to accept the moment as it is, that will be what you experience and what will be reflected in your life. You can understand this better if, when you are really angry and blaming others, you go to a mirror and see yourself reflected in it. Who are you pointing the finger at? What is your attitude toward yourself?

It doesn't matter what happened in our lives before; what matters is what we do today. What is the level of our consciousness, our thoughts and feelings? Are they a reflection of what we want to experience? Are they loving, caring, or peaceful? Or are they full of hate, resentment and judgment?

If you put your face close to a lake, you will see yourself reflected in it exactly as you are. It is the same with our emotions and thoughts, which are reflected in our own inner lake in the form of experiences, relationships, and the context of our present life.

Sometimes we are aware that this is the case, but we don't know how to change it or how to deal with it. But that is not as important as being honest with ourselves and recognizing that something inside us needs to be taken care of.

If you realize that when we are very happy and everything is going well for us, it is easy to feel responsible for having created these circumstances in our lives, but when they are not what we expected or even very difficult to digest, we unconsciously fill ourselves with excuses and blame others or the circumstances of life instead of observing our inner space, our lake or our waters. These emotional and mental patterns are reflected in the quality of our lives.

It is not there as a punishment because we are bad people or not doing right. There is no judgment; it is only with ourselves. We are here in this scenario to learn and evolve, and in that sense, our mistakes, or what warns us that they are not correct, are what teach us to refine and be better each time. Like a child learning to walk, it is not important how many times you fall or how many times you make mistakes, but rather that you get back up and keep trying until you walk naturally.

The more ability you have to separate yourself from these emotions and realize that they are just emotions and that you do not have to identify with them, the faster they can pass without creating any negative effects in your life.

Because really, you are like the sun that shines behind the clouds. And sometimes those clouds are so big and challenging that we identify with them, but those emotions, or thoughts, or beliefs are not who we really are. We are constantly evolving, and we can simply change them for others that are more in line with what we want to reflect in our lives. If we want our lives to be peaceful, kind, and happy, our thoughts, our actions, and our way of speaking and communicating must be.

Habits of Judgment and Criticism

Judgment plays havoc with the reflection that shows up in our life experiences, because if we are constantly judging ourselves and others, that is what will be expressed in our lives. We will undoubtedly have more and more reasons to be critical and judgmental, and we will continue to spend all of our energy doing so. We will continue to get caught up in the tangle of what we cannot understand unless we broaden our perspective.

But if at some point we decide that has been enough, we can reorder our thinking and allow kindness and compassion to do their work within us. Being very critical of yourself is a reflection that on some level you have stopped loving yourself, and the same thing happens with others, and that inevitably only makes you suffer.

You simply have to observe what is happening within you and love yourself again, treating yourself with respect, affection and compassion. Sometimes we demand that others respect us, but if we look at ourselves in the mirror, we will see that in most cases it is we who have stopped respecting ourselves. When you see it, when you observe it from a distance, without identifying with it, you can simply make the changes with your intention and regain that love for yourself.

The more difficult the situation you face, the more you have to practice it. Just water your seeds and eventually the garden will be filled with the beautiful experiences you want in your life, just as you envision them in your consciousness or even beyond.

BE THE WITNESS

Being a witness is a state in which there is no movement; it is a deep observation in which you do not intervene or participate. As if everything is happening outside of you. You are in the stands, watching yourself. To see your thoughts and emotions, but not from the point of view of the one who is experiencing them, but from the point of view of the one who is observing them, is a consciousness greater than your own identity. You are only a witness to what is happening, and you see the movement of thoughts, emotions, and everything else that requires your action.

However, your consciousness is present in a state that witnesses everything without being immersed in it. You can even go beyond this moment, beyond time and space. Like an ancient old tree that has witnessed continuous transformations, stages, constructions, wars, celebrations, meetings... Everything happens around it and it continues to provide shelter without participating in any of the scenes.

We can reach that level of awareness that keeps us connected to the present without being constantly moved by the comings and goings of our thoughts and emotions or what is happening around us, immersed in a higher level of *presence*. Movement and change do not affect us; we only flow with what does not change. That which remains beyond the circumstances and events of our lives. We are more than our impulses, reactions, opinions or beliefs.

We navigate the river of life, but there is something that keeps us eternal: Always in the background, observing without intervening or participating. This higher intelligence is what connects us to everything. The more we practice this state of witnessing and being aware of it, the more we have access to this intelligence, this source of love, peace and joy that we have all been able to experience and that we may have attributed to external circumstances, but that actually lives within us; it is our true nature; it is who we really are.

"If we could see the miracle of a single flower clearly, our whole life would change."—Buddha

Practice

Choose a place in nature where there is a large tree with extraordinary roots. It can be in a park or in the middle of nature, and you can take shelter there. Sit for a while and observe. Begin by observing your breathing and how deep it is.

Then observe your emotions and thoughts, but do not analyze them; just pay attention to what is happening. It is as if you were a child hiding for a while, and you can see everything, but nothing sees you.

Everything around you disappears: the sounds, the sensations that you perceive with your senses-everything is silent. There is just the tree and you. You merge with it. Its roots are your roots. Let nature guide you on this inner journey to yourself. To discover new things about yourself, just as a witness, without identifying yourself, listen to your own inner voice and allow it to show you or reveal something new about yourself, something you may not have considered. Something you have not yet discovered about yourself. You are like the ancient tree that seems to have all the answers. In this practice, where you are only the witness, can you connect with your inner guide?

Once you enter this sacred space of consultation and connection, make it empty, without expectations or trying to force a particular form of response.

When the connection you make with yourself is pure, without filters or packaging, it becomes easier, more fluid, and more effective.

We cannot enter a space of reflection, meditation, and inner guidance and at the same time want to control the answers or expect them to have a certain direction. If we really want inner guidance, we must be open to receiving it. The clearer our mental space is and the less we have a specific desire to fulfill our expectations, the deeper the result.

We notice it immediately because it is not a habitual response in us or in our daily way of thinking, but a more solid, deeper one. It is a broader guide that opens doors, that you tune into immediately because it resonates with you, and that really shows you the path that you can take with confidence, leaving behind everything that holds you in fear and does not allow you to move forward in freedom and fullness.

You don't have to believe it; just practice it and have a direct experience with your own inner guide. Let yourself go and merge with it. It is more about choosing and allowing yourself.

PATIENCE:
THE ART OF BEING PRESENT

There is a joke that says, “My God, give me patience, but now!" The funniest thing is that it usually a perfect reflection of how we usually behave.

Patience is like a good friend that we need to have by our side so that it can be there for us, especially in the moments when we need it most.

But like good friendships, we have to make sure that we cultivate it. If we do that, we can observe how this patience grows in us little by little, and there comes a time when it becomes solid and accompanies us naturally and spontaneously.

The most common, however, is that in everyday experience, we do not begin to value them until we realize that we do not have them. And it's strange, because the more we demand it, the further away it gets. It's like trying to catch a butterfly and it gets away, but if you stop trying to catch it, it just lands on you.

Patience is the same; the more we demand it, the more it moves away from us. It has to do with the natural rhythm and flow of life, synchronized with the rhythm we want to move in.

When we flow with life, we go at its pace, and everything works, even pleasantly surprising us and thinking, How is it possible that everything turned out well in the end? It's as if time stretched and, at the last moment, granted us a small extension until we did everything we needed to do and everything came out at the right time.

However, most of the time we want to demand our own rhythm, and the only thing that is reflected is that we ourselves are the ones who are out of time, looking at obstacles instead of flowing without resistance, and this only leads us to experience going against the current and to overcome more and more impediments.

People who are accustomed to meditating and using conscious breathing as a tool of help will use it when they need it because they are accustomed to experiencing that it is exactly what is needed when they feel they have lost their patience. Because if you do not do this, you are predisposed to creating more fear, which is nothing more than the anticipation of what is going to happen.

But if in that moment you are able to take your attention away from whatever is preoccupying you, recognize that you are anticipating yourself, and take a few minutes to observe your breathing and be aware of how to calm it down, you will immediately notice the effect it has on the end result. It is as if everything stops and returns to its synchronized rhythm; even your breathing becomes rhythmic and harmonious.

Then the right idea comes along, or a suggestion you hadn't thought of, or someone tells you something you hadn't even heard. And yet it is the answer to what you have been looking for. In general, you soften the energy of worry and anticipation, regain your power to be present, and attract more valuable options that would never have come to you otherwise.

Have you ever been in a situation where someone is walking behind you and pushing you to walk faster? How uncomfortable is that? In those cases, if we don't want to lose our rhythm, we move away and let it pass.

What life does to us in these cases is exactly the same; it withdraws so that we go our way alone. And then we realize that we are alone, carrying the weight of the world on our backs, returning to the position of victim of fate.

It is easier and more effective to align our inner rhythm to the rhythm of the moment.
Being patient does not mean being slow or settling, but rather knowing how to be in the right place at the right time, doing the right thing. It is adjusting your rhythm to the natural rhythm of flowing with what is presented to you in life. People who practice surfing get used to observing and adjusting the exact moment to catch the right wave that will carry them to shore.

For it is only in the present moment that everything happens and where all your power is. The space where all possibilities are latent, and the opportunity is there for you. Not for you to catch it or cling to it, but for it to find you and land on you like the butterfly. You just have to be patient and give it its time.

"When the fruit is ripe, it falls only from the tree."

And that is the moment when it is at its peak, ready to be tasted.

THE BEAUTY OF IMPERMANENCE

The impermanence that we cannot hold, control, or perpetuate in our small world is a blessing; it has an added value, even if our minds do not allow us to understand it at first. Because in realizing it, it takes us and forces us to go a little further than where our consciousness is.

Nothing is ours; nothing belongs to us. When we leave this world, we leave empty-handed, and that is a law that no one can ignore.

But the degree of trust and love that we offer in each moment, the consciousness that we imprint with our *presence*, with our attitude, with our fullness in that moment, is all that enriches and gives value to our lives and to those around us.
We enjoy every moment of the journey beyond the judgment of what we think it should be, totally surrendered to the implicit beauty of each

moment. We are full of love, and when we love, we love with all that we are, leaving nothing for tomorrow. This makes a big difference. Because then everything in our lives is printed and full of that love, that magic of the moment, fresh and spontaneous.

We are privileged: love is a treasure that expresses itself in our hearts from its own source or original unity, and when we let it flow through us, it fills us with blessings. We dwell in the realm of the sacred.

The sun shines every day, whether we are aware of it or not. Nothing stops flowing, growing, or expressing itself in the world. We join this flow of unconditional love when we respect and value that love within us, loving ourselves just as we are.

To savor the imperishable is the gift of a consciousness that has managed to transcend that which changes, transforms, and seems to disappear.

It never leaves us, and that is the 'great gift' of the one who has gone beyond forms, beyond the feeling of grief or loss. You realize that what you loved did not belong to you in a particular way, but you understand that this love is eternal; it does

not get lost or disappear; it just transforms into another higher level of consciousness. Pure love. Without division, without separation, imperishable, true.
It is a key that opens the door to the wisdom of an eternal mystery. Understanding that this love was and is much greater and deeper than anything you have ever experienced. It is sacred and enlightens everything. You are entering a new scenario, a scenario where everything is more real and purer because you have measured yourself with the greatness of love.

You will pass the test when you realize that nothing and no one can change what is real. What makes you love and be loved always remains intact; it is true and unique. It belongs to you, and you belong to it. That is what you are. Pure love expressing itself.

A deep peace floods your heart. There has been no error. Nothing is wrong. Everything has been as it should be.

Two lovers meeting and loving each other, nurturing and honoring that love beyond external circumstances, a love that does not justify itself, just is. No one else has to understand it. Only lovers are invited to the dance of love.

You cannot dance someone else's dance, but you can dance your own dance if you open your heart and dare to feel this love without conditions, keeping it pure first in yourself and then in what is loved.

There's nothing wrong with that; it's pure love. A love that, when it comes, you cannot reject because you are one with it. Everything disappears; only the fragrance and frequency of that love remains. The rest fades away, and when that true love becomes a reality in your life, even if it lasts a few seconds or a lifetime, there is no negotiation with this love; it does not allow anything to extinguish or slow it down because it is authentic and real. It is the truth upon which we walk and upon which the pillars of our lives are supported.

Supreme love is the love of that superior intelligence of the divine nature that unites us, sustains us, and gives meaning to our existence. The way that love is expressed in the world is very simple, but it varies. For some, it is divine and does not correspond to the physical plane of relationships with others; for others, it is the love of a couple, friendship, or family; for others, it is experienced through animals, places, work, passion, etc.

It is just love expressing itself. The more we bless it in our lives and surrender to it, the more able we are to experience it and feel what the honor of being in love is. You are aware that it is sacred, unique, and without equal. It does not change; it remains intact in your heart and is what gives meaning to who you are.

Feeling the imperishable nature of life makes us love everything we are in every moment, every day, knowing that we do not have to assume that tomorrow it will still be there in the same form.

Being willing to love without conditions means putting everything on the table. Even knowing the impermanent nature of life and knowing that there is no negotiation in the way we love, we just do it. We learn their language without letting ourselves burn out. Because the fire of love does not burn you, it only makes you more authentic and helps you discover the best in yourself.

We will have done it, and we will be loving without condition.

And that is something that belongs to us. We give everything. We love all that we have and are. We will have offered to be the eternal lovers who have no beginning and no end. You just love each other in the eternal weave of life. And then love shows you what you are. Boundless love comes when you have been brave enough not to label it or own it.

We do not ask or demand anything, but by loving in this way, love returns us, finds us and blesses us in its own expression and nature... Incalculable love is not indifferent.

When Lucia walked the path of transformation and loss, she realized that nothing had been in vain; on the contrary, she felt that love was more alive, even when it seemed impossible.

You can't go halfway, you have to put everything into it, you have to be all of yourself and melt into that love, and that love will show you what it means to be eternal, what can't change or die.

You have become an eternal lover. You are the *essence* of that love; it is who you are. Like a mirror, it will have shown you your nature and the divine quality that is within you...

DWELLING IN THE HEART: THE SACRED SPACE

Going down from continually living in the attic of the mind to dwelling in the space of the heart is a unique experience. The great conquest is not about anything external, but about our sacred place.

Then we feel that we have arrived; we are 'at home'. Beyond outer space! You don't have to travel great distances to reach it; it is always nests next to us, waiting for us to return with our conscience.

It is when the door of treasures opens. We embrace our breath, take a breath of life and know that everything is okay, no matter what.

Lucia always knew that when you find your place in the world, you cannot leave it, whether it be physically, a place to live, or in your heart. But she never understood why until this moment.

This place contains what you are; it is your *essence*, and it is not that you find it; it is that this *essence* or this place finds you.

It lives in you, but until you align with it, it cannot be expressed, and suddenly that is the moment or the space where everything comes together and is unique, brilliant, pure light.

Everything fits. All the pieces of the puzzle have come together, and you can understand, from your heart, who you are. Pure happiness.
In the words of *Ramana Maharshi*:

> *"Happiness is your nature. It is not wrong to desire it. What is wrong is seeking it outside when it is inside. Your duty is to be and not to be this or that."*

There it is, a moment when everything comes together so perfectly that it seems all the beaten paths have led you only to that moment...

We call it happiness. "I felt so happy." You have touched the sky of your own consciousness and the nature of your being. Your *essence*. What brings you there - the external circumstances - are not important; they do not count; just experiencing that moment is what matters. It gives it meaning and value.

You have arrived! Even if it is for a very brief moment of pure *presence*, you are in your home, the home where your heart lives, which is not physical but eternal.

And again, this impermanence that takes and moves what is not real, or all that is transitory, leaving only what is authentic... The face of truth that lives in each of us... That is who you are. Pure *essence*. The mistake has been in searching for it or trying to acquire it from the outside. It is present in everyone and can only be experienced.

The tests and challenges of life are only invitations or stages that force us to open our hearts enough to be willing to remember and allow this light that we all are and carry to be shown and reflected in the world... pure *radiance*.

It is so simple; it has always been there. We have covered our light with layers and layers of ignorance until it was lost in the confines of ourselves, just waiting for the right moment for us to decide to go inside, to be brave, and to love ourselves enough that all doubts fall and fade away. Then we realize that we no longer have to try to be something other than what we are; we can simply be.

We don't have to be better than we are; just remember what we are not. We are not our thoughts, which we have chosen to feed with our beliefs; we are not our ever-changing emotions; and we are not our habits.

We are eternal - that which remains and does not change. It is always available to us. It's that which does not allow change or transformation.

Our heart does not attend to time or space; it is free and eternal. Dwell in the realm of oneness, which never changes or can be lost. It is purity, happiness, and authenticity, and its language is honesty. Be honest with yourself and brave enough to embrace the *essence* that always remains in a state of wholeness.

Living in the space of the heart makes us happy, but this happiness is not external to us. It is not won, nor can we lose it. It is always there when we are present. We recognize the joy of being oneness in direct experience with ourselves.

There is no particular form or time for it. We are just We only dwell in his kingdom, the kingdom of the heart.

The eternal smile that has no face... It is a feeling; we smile with our heart. A universal frequency that unites us, makes us happy, real and alive.

PART III
RADIANCE

RADIANCE: SHINING OUR INNER LIGHT

When we shine, we are *radiance*. We are like tiny sun sparks reflected in water.

We reflect our *essence* in the world, which makes us unique and, at the same time, eternal and special. This light that is within us is our gift. It is the most authentic version of ourselves that connects us to the universe and to the source. Actually, we do not own it; it is not ours; we only reflect it. If we try to take it over with our ego or personality, it escapes us and loses its originality.

Many of the great artists in history who have connected with their *essence* and expressed it in the world have suffered great challenges in their lives, including a lack of resources, while today the value of their legacy is incalculable.

The purity of our gift, which remains unattainable for us, grows only when we express it, expand it, or share it without really getting involved.

We are all equally special. We all have a role to play and a gift to share with others that, when discovered and expressed, becomes unique and can change the lives of many.

It's not necessarily through art. When we can connect with our light, beauty, and vibration, it can be reflected in the most ordinary things: A fisherman going about his day with full awareness shines because of his simplicity. A child smiling at you with a full smile can change your day by reminding you of this *essence* that is also within you. This *essence* is connected to the whole universe, to the Absolute.

If we prepare a gift for someone and wrap it with the love of our *presence*, and even the smallest detail is full of meaning, the result cannot be compared to the most unique gift someone can give you, but it is devoid of detail and *presence*. Sometimes a simple flower, at the right moment, has more value than millions of bouquets put together. For authenticity is the added value in what we give or receive.

We do not need to be geniuses or artists to express our *essence* in the world; its value lies in the beauty of the simple, the small details. Those invisible threads that connect us to the divine and the sacred.

Practice:

During this day and in the days to come, as long as you are aware, observe what your attitude is in what you do and share with others. Whether it is your work, a conversation, or any activity of your day.

Is it impregnated with your *essence*? Or are you postponing the moment to share this gift, waiting for the right day or the perfect conditions you think are necessary to do it?

You can go even further with this invitation and observe what quality looks like in your relationship with yourself. What are your thoughts and feelings about yourself?

Loving and respecting yourself is a good example of using this gift, this quality of your thoughts and emotions with yourself. If you *radiate* a frequency of kindness and trust to yourself, you will imprint something of great value on your day and on everything you do - first to yourself, but also to others and through that to the whole world.

We cannot change what has happened in the past, nor do we know anything about an illusory future that, like the horizon, we will never reach. But we have the power to make this moment unique. To fill it with our *presence,* with our attention, with our love in those little things that, although simple, configure and constitute every moment of our day. Adjust or slow down the pace, not to stop doing what we have to do, but to do it authentically, fully, and full of *presence.*

What you think about yourself and what you pay attention to, nothing and no one can control... It belongs to you. It is your own indoor garden, and only you can decide what kind of flowers to plant and let grow. Sow those that make you feel good and then water them with your conscience and the quality that you put into what you do; the rest will take care of itself.

Sometimes you will have to add a little patience and a little compassion, but in the end you will shine and reflect to the world the truth that lives within you.

Our little oasis of freedom is only accessible to us. It is our inner space. Make that place a space of peace, a space of gratitude, and a space of love until it blossoms and *radiance* outward.

OUT OF THE MIND: GO WITH THE FLOW

Everything is simpler than it seems. Worry, anticipation and distraction consume all our energy. We become trapped in a series of repetitive and limiting thoughts that keep us in survival mode.

From this point on, we do not allow the new, fresh and pure *presence* of the moment to guide us. We have stopped going with the flow.

Everything becomes narrow and confined. We are not able to create anything from this place. We feel pressure and fear as if the limited scenario we are recreating, probably with the worst of the scenes, is the only possibility we have. We are back to duality. White or black, at the extremes. Actually, nothing is different on the outside; only our perception has been reduced and we are once again affected by conditioning.

Our mind is like a "Lego" game where you can create different original pieces with the pieces you have, but you cannot go off script because those are the pieces you have.

But when you connect and create from the heart, with passion and life force, your game is different because it is a language of pure creation without limits, like playing with clay or plasticine, with which you can create any shape without limits, from scratch. Or like the blank page waiting to be filled with the expression of your soul.

Whether it is a painting, writing, or 3D shape, whatever you can create with your imagination and creative ability goes beyond what has been created before. Like when you follow the instructions of a recipe that is written and you like it, but in the moment of preparing it, you start experimenting with the ingredients you have, with the textures and flavors, and in the end, the original recipe was only a source of inspiration for a new one, not yet written, but unique and hilariously genuine!...

But creation has no limits and goes as far as our consciousness can take it at that moment. Our conquests are not based on possessions, acquired experiences, or visited territories, but rather on where our consciousness has reached or expanded. That is our true conquest.

And it is no use making excuses or blaming others or external circumstances for where we have set our limits of thoughts and beliefs. But that is where our consciousness lives at that moment.

Our nature of "being free" reminds us of the teachings of the great masters, whose message is not lost in time.

We cannot change the world, but we can change the "little piece of consciousness" on which our vision of life is based or supported.

It's more about being mindful of what we pay attention to, where our consciousness is, and what we give power to. Know that when we are present-*presence*, we can shine in all our splendor -*radiance*.

If we realize that we are in survival mode and our perception has been reduced and has been affected by conditioning again, it is a good moment to breathe consciously, an invitation to take a deep breath.

Then we remember that we can choose, that we can relax for a moment, and that we can flow again with the current.

That's when we recover the power of our emotions. Every day and every moment has its own *essence*. Let's open ourselves to it and let it flow with life.

From a place of calm, we can choose with more dis-identification and balance; let's open ourselves to it, because by flowing with our way of thinking.

We can choose to have new thoughts that are much more constructive and kind to ourselves, thoughts that in themselves give us a breath of life and not the other way around.

We allow the best to come to us without giving it a name or shape, just by feeling good, comfortable, and creative again.

GRATITUDE: THE MEDICINE OF THE SOUL

Gratitude is the most valuable tool we have as human beings to instantly change our frequency from a state of sadness, depression or fatigue to one of joy, happiness and pure energy.

It is simple but very valuable to take just a few minutes a day for the pure joy of doing it, or in those moments when we notice that some energy is denser and has taken over us. It can help us to completely shift our state of mind and internal perception, and with that we can influence the course of our day and the reality that unfolds before us.

Gratitude has many levels, and as our ability to be grateful increases, so does our ability to receive. This does not depend on the number of times we say thank you, although that is a good start, but on the true depth with which we feel grateful.

It can range from a very basic level of trying to be polite because that is what is expected of us, to a complete lack of authenticity or value. Until you experience an immeasurable level of gratitude in complete communion, dissolving all separation, you become one with what you are grateful for.

It is like opening a little window and letting the light in, and each time you feel a little better, with a little more fresh air. Just by thinking about the things you are grateful for, your vibration changes and you begin to feel it.

If you are always stressed with your work or obligations, you will know that when you take a vacation, it is easier for you during those days, like a small oasis in your life, to relax and above all to "allow yourself" to vibrate at a calmer, more expansive and joyful frequency.

The same thing happens when we take our thoughts on "vacation" for a moment and focus for a few minutes on opening the door of gratitude within us and thinking about the things we feel blessed with until we really enter into the flow of this inexhaustible gratitude and its effects.

At first it may seem that we have no reason to be grateful, depending on our external environment.

As we begin to allow gratitude to flow into our consciousness and practice it every day, we can move from a trickle here and there of things we feel blessed about to fully entering that flow of gratitude.

Until we come to realize that the simplest or most obvious reasons are still valuable, reasons like breathing and allowing new oxygen to feed our lungs and keep us alive, it could be something obvious when it is not. It is still a miracle-the miracle of life.

The more you practice your list each day, the more reasons you will find to be grateful. It's as simple as that: Your attitude changes, taking your mind from the "vacation" state that you briefly allowed yourself to be in, to a state of true "grace" and blessing, where everything in your mind is influenced by this freshness and awareness of oneness.

When we connect with the true energy of gratitude, we realize that it requires no effort because it is natural to us; what requires real effort and takes all our energy is to be ungrateful.

A greater space is created in your thoughts, which are no longer so limited and constricted, and you begin to feel a little freer and to think big, in capital letters. The effect of this is that you in turn find more and more reasons to appreciate and be grateful for all the good that is in your life experience. Not just from the mind, but from your heart, feeling it and vibrating at a high frequency as a result of connecting with it.

WALKING YOUR WALK: HONORING WHO YOU ARE

The script is created by writing it as you walk your path. No matter how much the world shows you the path from the outside, you must walk it; no one can walk it for you.

Your successes and failures are not written. You write the script, but you can't just project it from your mind.

For ideas to become reality, action must be taken. No matter how much we can encompass with our imagination, we must allow it to materialize. This is where we take action with our choices, decisions, beliefs about what is possible or not, etc., to allow it to come true. It has more to do with what we open the door to and what we allow ourselves to access.

If we dream of being in a place, but then fill it with obstacles or excuses based on our thoughts, it is impossible for that place to reach us. Similarly, if we have an extraordinary idea or dream, but do not take the appropriate steps, actions, or beliefs, it is very difficult for us to see it come true. Any idea or project we can imagine with our mind is only a basic sketch to know where we are going. But then we have to 'feel' it and let the flame of its strength light our hearts.

In this way we will have activated it, and we will go from the world of ideas to matter to the physical. A child not only wishes with his imagination, but he is also able to feel and recreate each scene until he succeeds in making it come true.

We are ready to walk in the right direction and take the necessary steps—that is, the actions and the habits that allow our conscience to make it a reality.

We all know someone, or we can recognize it in ourselves, who is always dreaming, projecting with his mind a new idea, a new project, but never realizing it as a reality, never enjoying this direct experience...

It is powerful and comforting to realize our desires and dreams to fruition, not as something we postpone for a better time but as something we commit to until it becomes a reality. Later, we will realize that it was not having them in themselves that was important, but rather what led us to create them, what keeps our hearts awake and alive, embracing our incalculable potential and our own abilities.

When the time comes, we must take the appropriate steps and walk the path. It is not always easy, but if we remain faithful to what has motivated us to walk this path, all kinds of separations and limitations that keep it away from us will fade away, and we will advance much faster toward our goal or purpose.

The most beautiful thing is that there are no limits when we know that the page that represents life is always a blank page. A new canvas every day, which brings us the freshness of the present moment, even if we are not able to recognize it. Every day we write our script, and we imbue it with the quality that we decide, whether we are aware of it or not.

What we do at each step is the path itself, not where we are going. What makes the difference is how we perceive our life.

If we have no awareness of the present moment, of what we are doing, and of the energy we are projecting onto the stage with our thoughts and emotions, then nothing that happens could be created; it would just be frames of mental images waiting for someone to serve as the driving force, with their awareness and determination, to create the movement that generates the movie and the script.

That's when everything moves and makes sense. The plot itself is not important; it has no value in itself. Any experience we have in isolation is not predominant. It is important; only the journey as a whole gives it meaning, not our conscience.

We become entangled in every experience, every relationship, and every detail. The important thing is to take the necessary perspective to walk lighter, to understand and perceive reality with a broader understanding, like when you sit on the top of a mountain and can see the entire route of the trail. It is at that moment, when you understand that every experience, every decision has marked the path, the journey, that you have finally created your script.

The ability to enjoy is our ability to be present, the spontaneity and lightness of our own attitude... It is what makes us suffer or allows us to walk the path with serenity and gratitude beyond external circumstances. Because we remember that whatever we put our attention on, we illuminate it with our consciousness, we make room for it in our reality.

One of the first obstacles to overcome is not material, but the tendency to copy what others are doing instead of following your own heart. It is interesting to be inspired by others who have succeeded, but only as inspiration. Because if you get lost in it and all you want is the same thing that others have done, you will simply go down a dead-end road, and sooner or later you will realize that it was not yours either. You will be lost in the forms.

Instead, it is better to focus on the core of what inspires you and makes you feel good, and take that into your own territory. Wherever that takes you, it is always beyond what you could imagine with your mind or by copying what others are doing.

If you persist in what inspires you and motivates you to follow it, it will take you to a place where you will realize that you have transcended your own limitations. You will dwell in your own being because you will be doing what you were meant to do.

SILENCE:
BEYOND THE WORDS

Silence is like entering the cave of your inner sanctuary, the emerald of the heart. As you go deeper, like diving into the waters of the ocean of your own being, the language becomes purer and more authentic, communicating with yourself and with everything around you from a broader perspective than when you use spoken language.

The perception of time and space fades to a frequency where you remember the universal sound, the unity of everything, and the connection that, like in a circle, has no beginning or end, is not more important or less important, there are no comparisons, there is no separation or distinction... Everything is there. Silence communicates with us when we remember its language, a language that is eternal.

"In silence I express the language of my soul."

The doubts, the fears, the separation - they disappear. And as witnesses of eternity, we realize that what does not fit into a limited space is in a container with names, identifications, labels, or positions in life. Since all this is transitory, when we cross the confines of who we thought we were and the identity with that which we do not identify with, that is, when we are dwelling in the heart, we have ventured into our emerald, pure silence, pure truth.

Silence connects you to the soul of things, because when you connect to something from silence, from emptiness, without giving it a name, or a color, or a shape, its *truth* is revealed to you. It does not pay attention to interpretations, only to what it is, and it is familiar to you because deep down that truth is the same shared truth that lives in your heart.

It is a true communion. Everything becomes sacred when we submerge to the bottom of the sea and the superficial waves of words, noises, and concepts disappear to enter a new deep space that has always remained silent, although we do not appreciate it from the beginning.

Its silence and stillness are eternal and reveal to you the deepest mysteries—those that your heart holds. That's why you can recognize them, and that's why they are so valuable, because they contain your truth. It is the truth that waits in silence until it is heard.

Silence is expressed by our *presence*, not by words. It is not associated with external noise; it is internal, like a peaceful lake.

When we enter this inner state of stillness, we connect with frequencies that are very deep and healing. It is as if we are listening to the secrets of the universe that are waiting to be revealed. We can connect with everything that escapes our physical senses.

Have you ever heard the sound of ocean waves in a seashell, even when you are miles away from the ocean? Our interior is the same; it is connected to the original source, to the intelligence that is greater than us and always takes care of us. We just have to let it express itself and communicate.

Its message is peaceful, serene and always available. We just have to learn its language. A language without sound, which does not use words, but is expressed through our whole being.

THE ALCHEMY OF LIFE: REFINING OUR INNER GOLD

Alchemy is the knowledge of transforming matter, turning even metals into gold.

We also transform and evolve throughout our lives. It is about refining our inner gold through experience and direct contact with the truth that is shown to us.

It's about reconnecting with our *essence*. Allowing our gold to *radiate* its inner brilliance to the outside. This gold is not something that is added; it is something that we already are; it was already in us, but it has been covered and made opaque by our perceptions, beliefs, and life experiences, and we identify more and more with the character. This gold, or inner glow, fades and our innate value is weakened.

When we take back the reins again, we become alchemists, transforming everything we don't like about ourselves or our life experience into something purer and more authentic.
We give our lives a shine again, which little by little gives us back our joy, vitality, and luminosity. The brighter we shine, the more we remember our *essence*, and the easier it is for us to show it to the world.

The alchemy of life expresses itself and you discover that everything has been done the right way. There is no mistake. Every piece was equally important in creating our puzzle.

Every piece, every decision, every choice has contributed to making our light *radiate*. It's like there's a branch and then there's another branch and then there's another branch. A silhouette here and another one there, without understanding its meaning, until finally you can see the whole tree, where all those branches give it shape, and in that moment it becomes reality for you, and you understand everything.

We do things that have a different effect on our lives than we thought. But they were fundamental aspects of our transformation.

This inner gold, our *essence*, that which is eternal, is not lost, no matter how much the circumstances of our personal path lead us to forget it. It is always within our reach, for it is our true nature.

In reality, to a greater or lesser extent, we are all seekers of something that is missing. Like a piece that we haven't quite put together.

Perhaps it is something that you have been able to experience, as if there is something inside you that is still unanswered. Something that you still need to understand in order to know the full truth. There is something that still resists you and that you cannot access from the level of consciousness that you are at. And that leads you to seek. To want to know.

We are all these gold diggers. But not in a distant mountain, but in the search for our own inner gold; in reality we are looking for the brightness of our heart, the truth that remains motionless.

All those who have found and discovered the truth that lives within them should allow that *brilliance* to be reflected in the world. A light that knows no boundaries and illuminates everything around it. We call them enlightened, or masters, because they reflect the awakened wisdom that covers the veil of *ignorance*. And through their light we also remember. We remember that forgotten but common truth of our spirit that remains untouchable. And we connect with an inner sense of truth.

As soon as we glimpse that love or that inner light, the search stops because we recognize ourselves, and we *radiate* our truth.

We embrace what we are, we love each other, and we breathe the love we carry, which is unlimited and inexhaustible, and which grows and expands as we express it. That's when we settle into that eternal consciousness and navigate new waters of understanding.

Like a ring, when it is melted down to create another piece of jewelry, it is not the shape or the name we give it, but the gold itself, its *essence*, that remains. Likewise, in our search and transformation, there was nothing external to be found, but only the recognition of our most precious truth - the love that is and dwells within our true nature.

Only you, through your direct experience, can discover this truth within yourself. Only you can turn on that inner light with your faith, your attitude, and your practice. It is always dormant until you can turn it on and keep it on.

When you have remembered it and understood it with your heart, it will never go out. You will have awakened to your own truth. You are the alchemist who knows the secrets and mysteries of life. You have discovered your own inner brilliance and gold. You have known yourself.

TRUE LOVE

When we transcend the love of this or that, we enter into a complete connection with everything.

The great spiritual teachers have taught us to love ourselves. Their teachings are simple:
"Love everyone without distinction", "Serve everyone". And our response is usually, "Love everyone? How can I love and serve everyone equally?

There is no limit to the form and depth of loving ourselves, because then we discover that we are not separated from the source of love that we are, the pure love that is expressed within us, and from there, from ourselves, to the whole world.

We allow ourselves to be that; we merge with the true, limitless love that lives within each of us. We are this source of love and from this deep understanding we realize that we can love everyone without distinction- all people, animals, plants and all beings - the whole planet in full communion.

Our little inner world is revealed to us, and we understand our greatness, our true nature, which is not subject to this body or mind. We are free, we are eternal, and we can love without limits because we are the generators and bearers of that love. We no longer have to look for it in others; we no longer have to negotiate with love: "If you love me, I love you."

When we are with another, we share this love, we express it without limits, it is authentic and pure, and we recognize its *essence* in an infinite give and receive and intimate. An eternal dance that exceeds the personal or individual.

We are pure love, without beginning, without end, immeasurable, inexhaustible; the more we express it, the more our understanding of ourselves grows, and that makes us free, expansive, and happy.

Then it is easy for us to also love and serve others, because it is not us who do it; it is not the personage. It is our divine part expressing itself through us, through our actions, the way we think, and the way we feel, when we allow that love, beyond external circumstances, to express itself in the world.

Do not wait for the circumstances of your life to be this or that or for the perfect moment. Do not postpone the happiness and bliss that comes from loving yourself here and now as you are.

It doesn't matter what was done or what happened in the past. In this moment love yourself without anything having to be different than it is now. Love yourself and allow that love to expand in every cell, in every expression of yourself; love yourself beyond what you have ever allowed yourself to love.

Embrace your being; you are a fundamental part of this expression of love in the world.
It can only be expressed through you. And therein lies the great service that we are all destined to render to the world. It is not life that "owes" us anything, it is we who have the opportunity and the choice to express that gratitude to life for allowing us to be alive, for recognizing that love is, and being able to experience it within ourselves and express it in the world.

Love yourself here, now, without limits. And allow that love to dwell within you.

WINGS OF FREEDOM

This kind of flying or lifting does not require physical wings to fly. It is your conscience that elevates your mood and your spirit to unimaginable levels.

It is the recognition that our freedom does not depend on any external circumstances. We only rise beyond our own mental and emotional conditioning because we choose to do so. And we allow ourselves to shine and tune into a frequency that is not bound by time or space—formless, nameless: pure light, emptiness, silence, and eternity. We recognize ourselves with that which is greater than our physicality, which is already free and expansive, and we do this by setting our intention to tune into what we really are.

What we desire and long for in our hearts is not something external that we must achieve; it already lives in our consciousness and is therefore real. It is already within us because if it were not, there would be nothing to drive us to be, do, or have what we want.

Whether it becomes real on the physical plane or in matter does not depend on time; it only takes an instant. But how close or far we believe it is from us is what brings it closer or further away from our reality.

Our wings to be free are what we shelter with our conscience.

If you close your eyes for a moment, breathe deeply, and begin to generate peace, even in moments of stress or anxiety, that peace will take over. You have invited it with your intention and thought, and you have opened your emotional door to feel it fully.

You don't have to have reasons to be peaceful; just decide to experience that peace within yourself. The deeper you go into this little practice and the less effort you put into it, the more available you will be to experience that peace in yourself. Because it is who you are, and that is the reason why you feel good, expansive, and happy when you perceive it.

Freedom is not something we need to acquire because we are already free. Nothing, no one, and no circumstance can determine or control where we want our consciousness to be. What we give power to with our attention or way of thinking.

This is our personal journey, our individual path, where our efforts and habits must be focused on obtaining the maximum result.

If you smile in the face of adversity, your conscience indicates that you are free.

If, faced with the rain of intense and uncontrollable emotions, you open your umbrella and let them slide without penetrating you, you are free.

If, when you are tired and feel that you cannot go on or do not want to go on, you take another step forward, you are free.

If the circumstances around you are extreme and you have lost faith, but with the new dawn you are willing to try again, freedom continues with you.

And the scenario will eventually change and adapt to the frequency of freedom that you have imposed and chosen. Not because of any external circumstance, but because you have chosen it in your conscience.

There is no miracle or trick. It is your choice where you place your consciousness and attention to create the scenario that becomes reality for you.

You don't have to believe it, just experience it. Change your attitude towards the world or what surrounds you, and instantly reality will adjust to that frequency. Like a jelly that resonates with your vibration, it will move with your rhythm.

Each time you choose with your attitude how you want to feel, you will see for yourself how wide your wings are. Wings of freedom. Fly with your consciousness wherever you want to be.

And like a role-playing game, you will find yourself playing the role you have chosen down to the smallest detail —the true role that you were destined to play in this world and that only you can play.

FINAL CHAPTER

Dedicated to those who have lost their great love and have had to move on "with just a wing" in their hearts, continuing their journey of life with courage and bravery

Dance to your own song that has the melody of the divine, of the sacred, of what cannot be lost. Dance your song, even when you can't hear the music. Sing then and guide your feet that move silently, immersed in the universal sound.

Dance, dance, dance. It is the echo of music without sound—the eternal echo—that hurts to listen and know that we are also eternal. And I say it hurts because, in order to hear it, our false and imposter personality must disappear. It no longer has consistency when you can hear the verses of God in your heart; you can only sing you can only dance.

And in Lucia's words, directly expressed:

"When the music stopped for us, I followed the rhythm of our Love, I continued singing, remembering our Eternal melody. A sacred Love that resonates in the confines of existence, where we will always be.

Together, we recognized that love, and together we cared for it, protected it, and expressed it in the world. That truth that we proposed so many times and reminded others of:

"Don't stop dancing; don't stop. Love is the substance that unites the world, that unites all the pieces of our internal puzzle. Love lifts us up and makes us the best version of ourselves. We shine. We *radiate* and illuminate the world when we sing our melody."

It was then that Lucia remembered a Japanese technique called *'kintsugi'* whose simile they loved to use when they worked together in therapy and which consists of putting together pieces of highly valuable ceramics that have been broken, with a paste made of resin lacquer dusted with gold or another precious metal powder, and the final result acquires a much greater value than it originally had.

The same thing happens with our hearts, with the scars of some experiences in life, where we feel that our hearts have been broken into pieces, and through a process of transformation and awareness, including a lot of love and patience as basic ingredients, we overcome our own challenges.

And over time, we realize that those events that have marked us have, in turn, contributed to improving ourselves. As if time were in charge of uniting each of those broken pieces of new. The result is that we have transformed ourselves into someone much better than we were before.

Be who you really are, even if that means shedding everything that is not authentic about you or encouraging you to move in another direction.

Be brave; be free.

Because, as in the Japanese technique, the final result of the experience in life greatly exceeds the initial state that you could imagine.

We are passing through as guests of the Universe, but our piece is also important.

When we let love, without seeking anything in return, simply live fully in us, that is 'living eternally'. Because we become that *ESSENCE* that does not die; it only transforms. Love expressing itself. Pure consciousness.

Inspired by some words of Rumi:

"Beyond good and bad, there is a place,
we will always meet there."

www.ingramcontent.com/pod-product-compliance
Lightning Source LLC
LaVergne TN
LVHW010922110826
845149LV00013B/2446

* 9 7 8 1 9 6 2 9 8 4 0 8 9 *